MW01435761

GOD'S GREATEST BIBLE PROMISES OF BLESSING FOR YOUR LIFE

WHITAKER HOUSE

God's Greatest Bible Promises of Blessing for Your Life

Over 100 Scriptures from the King James Version Easy Read Bible (KJVER)

ISBN: 979-8-88769-332-3
eBook ISBN: 979-8-88769-333-0
Printed in the United States of America

Whitaker House
1030 Hunt Valley Circle New Kensington, PA 15068
www.whitakerhouse.com

Library of Congress Control Number: 2024922502

1 2 3 4 5 6 7 8 9 10 ш 31 30 29 28 27 26 25

CONTENTS

GOD PROMISES PHYSICAL BLESSINGS

GOD PROMISES MATERIAL BLESSINGS

GOD PROMISES TO...

KEEP HIS PROMISES

He is faithful that promised.

—Hebrews 10:23

God is not a man, that He should lie; neither the son of man, that He should repent: has He said, and shall He not do it? or has He spoken, and shall He not make it good?

—Numbers 23:19

Nevertheless My lovingkindness will I not utterly take from him,
nor allow My faithfulness to fail. My covenant will I not break, nor alter the thing that is gone out of My lips.

—Psalm 89:33–34

For all the promises of God in
[Jesus Christ] *are yea, and in Him*
Amen, to the glory of God by us.
—2 Corinthians 1:20

HEAR OUR PRAYERS

This is the confidence that we have in Him, that, if we ask any thing according to His will, He hears us: and if we know that He hear us, whatsoever we ask, we know that we have the petitions that we desired of Him.

—1 John 5:14–15

Behold, the LORD*'s hand is not shortened, that it cannot save; neither His ear heavy, that it cannot hear.*

—Isaiah 59:1

If My people, which are called by My name, shall humble themselves, and pray, and seek My face, and turn from their wicked ways; then will I hear from heaven, and will forgive their sin, and will heal their land.

—2 Chronicles 7:14

ANSWER OUR PRAYERS

Call to Me, and I will answer you, and show you great and mighty things, which you know not.

—Jeremiah 33:3

Therefore I say to you, What things soever you desire, when you pray, believe that you receive them, and you shall have them.

—Mark 11:24

If you abide in Me, and My words abide in you, you shall ask what you will, and it shall be done to you.

—John 15:7

GOD PROMISES SPIRITUAL BLESSINGS...

SALVATION

For God sent not His Son into the world to condemn the world; but that the world through Him might be saved.

—John 3:17

She shall bring forth a son, and you shall call His name JESUS: for He shall save His people from their sins.

—Matthew 1:21

If you shall confess with your mouth the Lord Jesus, and shall believe in your heart that God has raised Him from the dead, you shall be saved. For with the heart man believes to righteousness; and with the mouth confession is made to salvation.

—Romans 10:9–10

For by grace are you saved through faith;
and that not of yourselves:
it is the gift of God: not of works, lest
any man should boast.

—Ephesians 2:8–9

NEW LIFE

Therefore we are buried with Him by baptism into death: that like as Christ was raised up from the dead by the glory of the Father, even so we also should walk in newness of life.

—Romans 6:4

Who His own self bore our sins in His own body on the tree, that we, being dead to sins, should live to righteousness: by whose stripes you were healed.

—1 Peter 2:24

Therefore if any man be in Christ, he is a new creature: old things are passed away; behold, all things are become new.

—2 Corinthians 5:17

A new heart also will I give you,
and a new Spirit will I put within you:
and I will take away the stony heart
out of your flesh,
and I will give you a heart of flesh.
—Ezekiel 36:26

I am crucified with Christ: nevertheless I live; yet not I, but Christ lives in me: and the life which I now live in the flesh I live by the faith of the Son of God, who loved me, and gave Himself for me.

—Galatians 2:20

FREEDOM

For sin shall not have dominion over you: for you are not under the law, but under grace.

—Romans 6:14

There is therefore now no condemnation to them which are in Christ Jesus, who walk not after the flesh, but after the Spirit. For the law of the Spirit of life in Christ Jesus has made me free from the law of sin and death.

—Romans 8:1–2

If the Son therefore shall make you free, you shall be free indeed.

—John 8:36

FORGIVENESS

Blessed is he whose transgression is

forgiven, whose sin is covered.

Blessed is the man to whom the Lord

imputes not iniquity,

and in whose spirit there is no guile.

—Psalm 32:1–2

In whom we have redemption through
His blood, the forgiveness of sins,
according to the riches of His grace.
—Ephesians 1:7

I, even I, am He that blots out your transgressions for My own sake, and will not remember your sins.

—Isaiah 43:25

If we confess our sins, He is faithful and just to forgive us our sins, and to cleanse us from all unrighteousness.

—1 John 1:9

RIGHTEOUSNESS

For He has made Him to be sin for us,
who knew no sin; that we might be made
the righteousness of God in Him.
—2 Corinthians 5:21

For if by one man's offense death reigned by one; much more they which receive abundance of grace and of the gift of righteousness shall reign in life by One, Jesus Christ.

—Romans 5:17

If Christ be in you, the body is dead because of sin; but the Spirit is life because of righteousness.

—Romans 8:10

THE HOLY SPIRIT

I will pray the Father, and He shall give you another Comforter, that He may abide with you for ever; even the Spirit of truth; whom the world cannot receive, because it sees Him not, neither knows Him: but you know Him; for He dwells with you, and shall be in you.

—John 14:16–17

But you shall receive power, after that the Holy Ghost is come upon you: and you shall be witnesses to Me both in Jerusalem, and in all Judaea, and in Samaria, and to the uttermost part of the earth.

—Acts 1:8

Then Peter said to them, Repent, and be baptized every one of you in the name of Jesus Christ for the remission of sins, and you shall receive the gift of the Holy Ghost. For the promise is to you, and to your children, and to all that are afar off, even as many as the Lord our God shall call.

—Acts 2:38–39

HIS WORD

He answered and said, It is written,
Man shall not live by bread alone,
but by every word that proceeds out of
the mouth of God.
—Matthew 4:4

For the word of God is quick,
and powerful, and sharper than any
two-edged sword, piercing even to the
dividing asunder of soul and spirit,
and of the joints and marrow,
and is a discerner of the thoughts and
intents of the heart.
—Hebrews 4:12

So shall My word be that goes forth out of My mouth: it shall not return to Me void, but it shall accomplish that which I please, and it shall prosper in the thing whereto I sent it.

—Isaiah 55:11

DELIVERANCE FROM EVIL

The Lord shall deliver me from every evil work, and will preserve me to His heavenly kingdom: to whom be glory for ever and ever. Amen.

—2 Timothy 4:18

For I am persuaded, that neither death, nor life, nor angels, nor principalities, nor powers, nor things present, nor things to come, nor height, nor depth, nor any other creature, shall be able to separate us from the love of God, which is in Christ Jesus our Lord.

—Romans 8:38–39

Because you have made the LORD, which is my refuge, even the Most High, your habitation; there shall no evil befall you, neither shall any plague come near your dwelling. For He shall give His angels charge over you, to keep you in all your ways.

—Psalm 91:9–11

HIS PRESENCE

Behold, I stand at the door, and knock: if any man hear My voice, and open the door, I will come in to him, and will sup with him, and he with Me.

—Revelation 3:20

Yea, though I walk through the valley of the shadow of death, I will fear no evil: for You are with me; Your rod and Your staff they comfort me.

—Psalm 23:4

Lo, I am with you always, even to the end of the world.

—Matthew 28:20

SPIRITUAL GROWTH

Being confident of this very thing,
that He which has begun
a good work in you will perform it until
the day of Jesus Christ.
—Philippians 1:6

But we all, with open face beholding as
in a glass the glory of the Lord,
are changed into the same image from
glory to glory, even as by the
Spirit of the Lord.

—2 Corinthians 3:18

His divine power has given to us all
things that pertain to life and godliness,
through the knowledge of Him that has
called us to glory and virtue.

—2 Peter 1:3

SPIRITUAL GIFTS

See, I have...filled him with the Spirit of God, in wisdom, and in understanding, and in knowledge, and in all manner of workmanship, to devise cunning works, to work in gold, and in silver, and in brass, and in cutting of stones, to set them, and in carving of timber, to work in all manner of workmanship.

—Exodus 31:2–5

So we, being many, are one body in Christ, and every one members one of another. Having then gifts differing according to the grace that is given to us, whether prophecy, let us prophesy according to the proportion of faith; or ministry, let us wait on our ministering: or he that teaches, on teaching; or he that exhorts, on exhortation: he that gives, let him do it with simplicity; he that rules, with diligence; he that shows mercy, with cheerfulness.

—Romans 12:5–8

For the gifts and calling of God are without repentance.

—Romans 11:29

TRUTH

For the truth's sake, which dwells in us,

and shall be with us for ever.

Grace be with you, mercy, and peace,

from God the Father, and from the Lord

Jesus Christ, the Son of the Father,

in truth and love.

—2 John 1:2–3

For the fruit of the Spirit is in all goodness and righteousness and truth.

—Ephesians 5:9

Then said Jesus...If you continue in My word, then are you My disciples indeed; and you shall know the truth, and the truth shall make you free.

—John 8:31–32

LOVE

As the Father has loved Me, so have I loved you: continue you in My love.

—John 15:9

But God commends His love toward us,
in that, while we were yet sinners,
Christ died for us.
—Romans 5:8

In this was manifested the love of God toward us, because that God sent His only begotten Son into the world, that we might live through Him. Herein is love, not that we loved God,
but that He loved us, and sent His Son to be the propitiation for our sins.

—1 John 4:9–10

JOY

You will show me the path of life:
in Your presence is fullness of joy;
at Your right hand there are pleasures
for evermore.

—Psalm 16:11

These things have I spoken to you, that My joy might remain in you, and that your joy might be full.

—John 15:11

The angel said to them, Fear not: for, behold, I bring you good tidings of great joy, which shall be to all people.

—Luke 2:10

PEACE

The Lord will give strength to His people; the Lord will bless His people with peace.

—Psalm 29:11

You will keep him in perfect peace,
whose mind is stayed on You: because he
trusts in You.

—Isaiah 26:3

The peace of God, which passes all understanding, shall keep your hearts and minds through Christ Jesus.

—Philippians 4:7

Therefore being justified by faith, we have peace with God through our Lord Jesus Christ.

—Romans 5:1

Peace I leave with you, My peace I give to you: not as the world gives, give I to you. Let not your heart be troubled, neither let it be afraid.

—John 14:27

HOPE

To whom God would make known what is the riches of the glory of this mystery among the Gentiles; which is Christ in you, the hope of glory.

—Colossians 1:27

[We] *rejoice in hope of the glory of God. . . . And hope makes not ashamed; because the love of God is shed abroad in our hearts by the Holy Ghost which is given to us.*

—Romans 5:2, 5

For You are my hope, O Lord God:
You are my trust from my youth.
—Psalm 71:5

Now the God of hope fill you with all joy and peace in believing, that you may abound in hope, through the power of the Holy Ghost.
—Romans 15:13

Blessed be the God and Father of our Lord Jesus Christ, which according to His abundant mercy has begotten us again to a lively hope by the resurrection of Jesus Christ from the dead.

—1 Peter 1:3

GOD PROMISES FUTURE BLESSINGS...

ETERNAL LIFE

For God so loved the world, that He
gave His only begotten Son,
that whosoever believes in Him should
not perish, but have everlasting life.
—John 3:16

This is the record, that God has given to us eternal life, and this life is in His Son. He that has the Son has life; and he that has not the Son of God has not life.

—1 John 5:11–12

For the wages of sin is death; but the gift of God is eternal life through Jesus Christ our Lord.

—Romans 6:23

Verily, verily, I say to you, He that hears My word, and believes on Him that sent Me, has everlasting life, and shall not come into condemnation; but is passed from death to life.

—John 5:24

He that loves his life shall lose it; and he that hates his life in this world shall keep it to life eternal.

—John 12:25

LIFE AFTER DEATH

But if the Spirit of Him that raised up Jesus from the dead dwell in you, He that raised up Christ from the dead shall also quicken your mortal bodies by His Spirit that dwells in you.

—Romans 8:11

In a moment, in the twinkling of an eye, at the last trump: for the trumpet shall sound, and the dead shall be raised incorruptible, and we shall be changed. For this corruptible must put on incorruption, and this mortal must put on immortality.

—1 Corinthians 15:52–53

Jesus said to her, I am the resurrection,
and the life: he that believes in Me,
though he were dead, yet shall he live:
and whosoever lives and believes in Me
shall never die. Believe you this?

—John 11:25–26

JESUS'S RETURN

For the Lord Himself shall
descend from heaven with a shout, with
the voice of the archangel,
and with the trump of God....So shall
we ever be with the Lord.
—1 Thessalonians 4:16–17

For as the lightning comes out of the east, and shines even to the west; so shall also the coming of the Son of man be.…And then shall appear the sign of the Son of man in heaven: and then shall all the tribes of the earth mourn, and they shall see the Son of man coming in the clouds of heaven with power and great glory.

—Matthew 24:27, 30

This same Jesus, which is taken up from
you into heaven, shall so
come in like manner as you have seen
Him go into heaven.

—Acts 1:11

HEAVEN

For here have we no continuing city,
but we seek one to come.
—Hebrews 13:14

And I John saw the holy city, new Jerusalem, coming down from God out of heaven, prepared as a bride adorned for her husband. And I heard a great voice out of heaven saying, Behold, the tabernacle of God is with men, and He will dwell with them, and they shall be His people, and God Himself shall be with them, and be their God.

—Revelation 21:2–3

Jesus said to him, Verily I say to you,
Today shall you be with Me in paradise.
—Luke 23:43

GOD PROMISES PERSONAL BLESSINGS...

STRENGTH

Trust you in the Lord for ever:
for in the Lord JEHOVAH is
everlasting strength.
—Isaiah 26:4

The Lord is my strength and my shield;
my heart trusted in Him,
and I am helped: therefore my heart
greatly rejoices; and with my song will I
praise Him.
—Psalm 28:7

Finally, my brethren, be strong in the Lord, and in the power of His might.

—Ephesians 6:10

But they that wait upon the Lord *shall renew their strength; they shall mount up with wings as eagles; they shall run, and not be weary; and they shall walk, and not faint.*

—Isaiah 40:31

I can do all things through Christ which strengthens me.

—Philippians 4:13

CONFIDENCE

In the fear of the LORD is strong confidence: and his children shall have a place of refuge.

—Proverbs 14:26

For thus says the Lord God, *the Holy One of Israel; In returning and rest shall you be saved; in quietness and in confidence shall be your strength.*
—Isaiah 30:15

Be not afraid of sudden fear, neither of the desolation of the wicked, when it comes. For the Lord *shall be your confidence, and shall keep your foot from being taken.*
—Proverbs 3:25–26

WISDOM

The fear of the Lord *is the beginning of wisdom: and the knowledge of the holy is understanding.*

—Proverbs 9:10

Blessed be the name of God for ever and ever: for wisdom and might are His... He gives wisdom to the wise, and knowledge to them that know understanding: He reveals the deep and secret things: He knows what is in the darkness, and the light dwells with Him.

—Daniel 2:20–22

If any of you lack wisdom, let him ask of God, that gives to all men liberally, and upbraids not; and it shall be given him.

—James 1:5

INSTRUCTION

All scripture is given by inspiration of God, and is profitable for doctrine, for reproof, for correction, for instruction in righteousness: that the man of God may be perfect, thoroughly furnished to all good works.

—2 Timothy 3:16–17

He that refuses instruction despises his own soul: but he that hears reproof gets understanding. The fear of the LORD *is the instruction of wisdom; and before honor is humility.*

—Proverbs 15:32–33

Hear counsel, and receive instruction,
that you may be wise in your latter end.
There are many devices in a man's heart;
nevertheless the counsel of the L*ORD*,
that shall stand.
—Proverbs 19:20–21

GUIDANCE

I will instruct you and teach you
in the way which you shall go: I will
guide you with My eye.

—Psalm 32:8

If I take the wings of the morning, and dwell in the uttermost parts of the sea; even there shall your hand lead me, and Your right hand shall hold me.

—Psalm 139:9–10

The Lord is my shepherd; I shall not want....He leads me in the paths of righteousness for His name's sake.

—Psalm 23:1, 3

SUCCESS

Believe in the L*ORD your God, so shall you be established; believe His prophets, so shall you prosper.*

—2 Chronicles 20:20

In all your ways acknowledge Him, and
He shall direct your paths.
—Proverbs 3:6

Commit your works to the Lord, *and*
your thoughts shall be established.
—Proverbs 16:3

HONOR

The Lord says,…Them that honor Me
I will honor, and they that despise Me
shall be lightly esteemed.
—1 Samuel 2:30

Because he has set his love upon Me, therefore will I deliver him....He shall call upon Me, and I will answer him: I will be with him in trouble; I will deliver him, and honor him.

—Psalm 91:14–15

The fear of the L*ORD* *is the instruction of wisdom; and before honor is humility.*

—Proverbs 15:33

SATISFACTION

[The Lord] *satisfies your mouth with good things; so that your youth is renewed like the eagle's.*

—Psalm 103:5

Jesus said to them, I am the bread of life:
he that comes to Me shall never hunger;
and he that believes on Me
shall never thirst.

—John 6:35

Oh that men would praise the LORD for His goodness, and for His wonderful works to the children of men! For He satisfies the longing soul, and fills the hungry soul with goodness.

—Psalm 107:8–9

COMFORT

In the multitude of my thoughts within me Your comforts delight my soul.

—Psalm 94:19

Blessed be God, even the Father of our Lord Jesus Christ, the Father of mercies, and the God of all comfort; who comforts us in all our tribulation, that we may be able to comfort them which are in any trouble, by the comfort wherewith we ourselves are comforted of God.

—2 Corinthians 1:3–4

Blessed are they that mourn: for they shall be comforted.

—Matthew 5:4

YOUR HEART'S DESIRE

Delight yourself also in the Lord; and He shall give you the desires of your heart.

—Psalm 37:4

The Lord hear you in the day of trouble....Grant you according to your own heart, and fulfill all your counsel.

—Psalm 20:1, 4

A new heart also will I give you, and a new Spirit will I put within you: and I will take away the stony heart out of your flesh, and I will give you a heart of flesh.

—Ezekiel 36:26

FAMILY BLESSINGS

All your children shall be taught of the Lord; and great shall be the peace of your children.

—Isaiah 54:13

Observe and hear all these words which I command you, that it may go well with you, and with your children after you for ever, when you do that which is good and right in the sight of the Lord *your God.*

—Deuteronomy 12:28

Train up a child in the way he should go:

and when he is old,

he will not depart from it.

—Proverbs 22:6

GOD PROMISES PHYSICAL BLESSINGS...

HEALTH

For I will restore health to you,
and I will heal you of your wounds,
says the Lord.
—Jeremiah 30:17

The L*ORD* *shall guide you continually, and satisfy your soul in drought, and* [give strength to] *your bones: and you shall be like a watered garden, and like a spring of water, whose waters fail not.*

—Isaiah 58:11

Because you have made the Lord, which is my refuge, even the Most High, your habitation; there shall no evil befall you, neither shall any plague come near your dwelling.

—Psalm 91:9–10

HEALING

Bless the Lord, O my soul,
and forget not all His benefits:
Who forgives all your iniquities;
who heals all your diseases.
—Psalm 103:2–3

Jesus went about all Galilee, teaching in their synagogues, and preaching the gospel of the kingdom, and healing all manner of sickness and all manner of disease among the people.

—Matthew 4:23

He was wounded for our transgressions,
He was bruised for our iniquities:
the chastisement of our peace was upon
Him; and with His stripes
we are healed.

—Isaiah 53:5

SAFETY

The Lord is my rock, and my fortress, and my deliverer; my God, my strength, in whom I will trust; my buckler, and the horn of my salvation, and my high tower.

—Psalm 18:2

I will both lay me down in peace, and sleep: for You, Lord, only make me dwell in safety.

—Psalm 4:8

He that dwells in the secret place of the Most High shall abide under the shadow of the Almighty. I will say of the Lord, He is my refuge and my fortress: my God; in Him will I trust.

—Psalm 91:1–2

PROTECTION

The Lord is your keeper: the Lord is your shade upon your right hand. The sun shall not smite you by day, nor the moon by night. The Lord shall preserve you from all evil: He shall preserve your soul. The Lord shall preserve your going out and your coming in from this time forth, and even for evermore.

—Psalm 121:5–8

Surely He shall deliver you from the
snare of the fowler,
and from the noisome pestilence. He
shall cover you with His feathers, and
under His wings shall you trust: His
truth shall be your shield and buckler.
—Psalm 91:3–4

For who is God save the Lord?
or who is a rock save our God?
It is God that girds me with strength,
and makes my way perfect.
—Psalm 18:31–32

LONG LIFE

Because he has set his love upon Me....
With long life will I satisfy him, and
show him My salvation.
—Psalm 91:14, 16

The fear of the L*ORD* *is the beginning of wisdom: and the knowledge of the holy is understanding. For by me your days shall be multiplied, and the years of your life shall be increased.*

—Proverbs 9:10–11

Honor your father and mother; (which is the first commandment with promise;) that it may be well with you, and you may live long on the earth.

—Ephesians 6:2–3

CHILDREN

Your wife shall be as a fruitful vine by the sides of your house: your children like olive plants round about your table.

—Psalm 128:3

Lo, children are a heritage of the LORD*:*
and the fruit of the womb is His reward.
As arrows are in the hand of a mighty
man; so are children of the youth.
Happy is the man that has his quiver
full of them.
—Psalm 127:3–5

He makes the barren woman
to keep house, and to be a joyful mother
of children.
—Psalm 113:9

GOD PROMISES MATERIAL BLESSINGS...

ABUNDANCE

My God shall supply all your need according to His riches in glory by Christ Jesus.

—Philippians 4:19

For the LORD God is a sun and shield: the LORD will give grace and glory: no good thing will He withhold from them that walk uprightly.

—Psalm 84:11

O fear the LORD, you His saints: for there is no want to them that fear Him. The young lions do lack, and suffer hunger: but they that seek the LORD shall not want any good thing.

—Psalm 34:9–10

PROSPERITY

Keep therefore the words of this covenant and do them, that you may prosper in all that you do.

—Deuteronomy 29:9

Blessed is every one that fears the L*ORD*; *that walks in His ways. For you shall eat the labor of your hands: happy shall you be, and it shall be well with you.*

—Psalm 128:1–2

Blessed is the man that walks not in the counsel of the ungodly....But his delight is in the law of the Lord*; and in His law does he meditate day and night. And he shall be like a tree planted by the rivers of water, that brings forth his fruit in his season; his leaf also shall not wither; and whatsoever he does shall prosper.*

—Psalm 1:1–3

FOOD

I have been young, and now am old; yet have I not seen the righteous forsaken, nor his seed begging bread.

—Psalm 37:25

Therefore I say to you, Take no thought for your life, what you shall eat, or what you shall drink....Is not the life more than meat...? Behold the fowls of the air: for they sow not, neither do they reap, nor gather into barns; yet your heavenly Father feeds them. Are you not much better than they?

—Matthew 6:25–26

[The Lord] *executes judgment for the oppressed* [and] *gives food to the hungry.*

—Psalm 146:6–7

HARVEST

If you walk in My statutes, and keep My commandments, and do them;
then I will give you rain in due season,
and the land shall yield her increase,
and the trees of the field shall yield their fruit. And your threshing shall reach to the vintage, and the vintage shall reach to the sowing time: and you shall eat your bread to the full,
and dwell in your land safely.

—Leviticus 26:3–5

Then shall He give the rain of your seed, that you shall sow the ground with; and bread of the increase of the earth, and it shall be fat and plenteous.

—Isaiah 30:23

He causes the grass to grow for the cattle, and herb for the service of man: that he may bring forth food out of the earth.

—Psalm 104:14